Photo by Richard Bram

A scene from the Stage One: The Louisville Children's Theatre production of "Dogbrain." Set design by Daniel S. Mangan.

DOGBRAIN

A Play for Children

BY MICHAEL WELLER

★

★

DRAMATISTS
PLAY SERVICE
INC.

DOGBRAIN was originally commissioned by
Stage One: The Louisville Children's Theatre,
as part of the New Generation Play Project,
funded by grants from the National Endowment for the Arts,
the Lila Wallace-Readers Digest Fund, the Children's Theatre Foundation
and the Robert E. Black Memorial Trust.

DOGBRAIN was commissioned by Stage One: The Louisville Children's Theatre (Moses Goldberg, Artistic Director; M. Christopher Boyer, Managing Director) at Actors Theatre of Louisville, in Louisville, Kentucky, and received its world premiere there on April 14, 1996. It was directed by Moses Goldberg; the set design was by Daniel S. Mangan; the costume design was by Donna E. Lawrence; the lighting and sound designs were by Jen Groseth; and the stage manager was Leslie Oberhausen. The cast was as follows:

NICHOLAS .... Jeremy Tow
THOMAS .... Alex Ward
MISS HARMONY. .... Katie Blackerby
MOM .... Anita Wittenberg
DAD .... Joel Weible
DOGBRAIN .... Karen Sabo
GOODYBAGS .... John Hedges
GERMAN LEOPARD .... Laura Parsons
BAG LADY .... Debra Macut

DOGBRAIN

A playground.

The noise of a children's schoolyard. Nicholas, age 6, runs on as if he's being chased by someone, which he's not.

He climbs to the highest place he can find and looks around. No one appears. He calls out:

NICK. HEY ... LOOK AT *ME,* EVERYONE. I'M NICHOLAS. I'M KING OF EVERYTHING. I'M KING OF THIS PLAYGROUND. I'M KING OF ADVENTURE.

(AUDIENCE PARTICIPATION VERSION.)

(Nick continues.) AND I CAN TRAVEL ANYWHERE I WANT. ALL I NEED IS SOMETHING TO RIDE ON. *(He can't think what. He appeals to the audience.)* LET ME SEE, WHAT CAN I RIDE ON? *(Wait for answers — bike, car, plane, train, etc. — for each suggestion he asks.)* HOW DOES A *(Bike, car, plane, train, etc.)* GO? SHOW ME!!! *(As audience members imitate a vehicle, so does Nicholas, until:)* HEY, LOOK AT THIS COOL TRAIN ... *(Climbs aboard.)* CHOO-CHOO ... *(Enter Tom. He's four.)*

(NON-PARTICIPATION VERSION.)

NICK. *(Finishing his speech.)* ... I'M KING OF THIS TRAIN ... CHOO-CHOO-CHOO ... *(Enter Tom. He's four.)* Hey, Tommy, you want to ride on my train? It can go anywhere; Mars, Oyster Bay, Dogville.

TOM. There's no Dogville.

NICK. Of course there is. Where do you think dogs come from?

TOM. Bigger dogs?

NICK. But where do the *bigger* dogs come from? *(Tom wonders about this.)* Dogville, of course! Want to see it? I'll take you there; come on —

TOM. 'Kay. *(Tom stands high beside Nick, who is happy now that he has a playmate.)*

NICK. All aboard!!! Cool train, huh? Ready, get set, *(Train noise.)* KSSHHHHH!!!

TOM. Can I drive?

NICK. No, 'cause you don't know where Dogville is. KSSHHHH!!!

TOM. I'll drive next time after you show me.

NICK. No, 'cause I'm king of this train and the rule is I drive. KSSHHHH, CHOO-CHOO …

TOM. That's a dumb rule. I'm not playing. *(Tom starts to leave.)*

NICK. You can't get off, we're moving really fast, "Next stop, Dogville …"

TOM. There's no such place. *(Nick grabs him.)*

NICK. Don't leave the train, you'll get hurt.

TOM. LET ME GO!!!

NICK. You have to stay here because you're my brother.

TOM. That doesn't mean I'm your friend … *(Nick hits him. All "freeze." Miss Harmony enters with Nick's Mom and they sit. Nick and Tom "unfreeze" and stand nearby. We are now in …)*

Miss Harmony's office.

MISS HARMONY. But why did you *hit* him, Nicholas?

NICK. He was trying to get off the train, Miss Harmony.

TOM. It was just a stupid game.

MISS HARMONY. Thomas, we mustn't use hurt-words like *stupid.*

TOM. It was just a pretend train.

NICK. It was for real and we were going over a river with sharks and alligators and they'd eat him to death if he got off the train.

TOM. *(Sotto voce.)* Stupid!

MOM. Nicholas, it was not a for-real train. You were playing a game and got carried away, didn't you.

TOM. And I didn't want to play and he hit me, mom!

NICK. He said he's not my friend.

MISS HARMONY. Ahah! I think we got to the bottom of this. Tom didn't want to play his game, and when he insisted, you got upset and used a hurt-word. *(Nick and Tom exchange a look, then nod at Miss Harmony, settling for her summation. Mom is distracted.)*

MOM. It's their first day of school, and we just moved to the neighborhood, you know how *that* is. Plus Thomas has a birthday coming up and Nicholas is a little jealous, I suppose. Plus I just got a big promotion at work, so I'm not at home as much as I used to be ... Nick is a sweet boy, he just has a very active imagination.

MISS HARMONY. Self-control is what we have to stress. Nicholas, Thomas, please apologize to each other.

NICK. Sorry.

TOM. Sorry.

MISS HARMONY. Now go out in the hall while I talk to your mother; and I want both of you to think of ways to work out your differences without hurt-words and physical aggression, okay? *(Nick and Tom go. When they're out of sight, Tom sticks out his tongue and Nick hits him.)*

TOM. Aaaargh!!! *(Mom runs out into the hallway. Nick looks perplexed by his own action. To Mom.)* He hit me!

MOM. NICHOLAS!!! *("Freeze." Miss Harmony leaves. Dad and Nick and Tom sit at the dinner table. We are now in their ...)*

Dining room.

Mom serves dinner. Nick and Tom quietly irritate each other while Mom and Dad try to talk.

MOM. It's not as if this is something new —

DAD. I never said it was —

MOM. That's exactly what you've been saying, that he's

TOM. *(Sing-song.)* I'm having a birthday, you can't come to the party...!

NICK. Shut up, Tom.

having trouble adjusting because of the move, then I have to go into school and explain all this when I don't even believe it myself, I mean why is it *me* that has to leave work in the middle of the day and deal with problems at school —

DAD. If you want *me* to leave work I'll be happy to —

MOM. That's not the point.

DAD. Then what *is* the point?

TOM. You can't say shut up, that's bad.

NICK. Shut your stupid face, buttbrain.

TOM. I don't have to.

NICK. Yes you do.

TOM. You can't make me, I'm almost five, you're not the king of me any more. *(Nick kicks him under the table.)* Mom, he kicked me!

NICK. Liar!!!

MOM. THAT'S *ENOUGH* YOU TWO. Can't we get through one entire meal in peace. And if I have to leave work in the middle of the day one more time.... You're six years old, for goodness sake.

TOM. Not me. I'm four an a half and two halves.

NICK. You're a great big mistake is what you are! *(Dad is chuckling quietly to himself.)*

MOM. I don't see anything funny about this.

DAD. Four and a half and two halves ... that's funny!

NICK. *(To Tom.)* There's no such thing, stupid-Tom pee-pee head!

MOM. *(Explodes.)* STOP IT, JUST STOP IT. *(To Dad.)* Why do you sit there encouraging them? I have to do *everything* around here, clean, cook, organize his birthday party, plus work all day so we can afford that school.... Why do I even bother, why don't I just sleep late so they fire me and we lose our house and end up on the streets with a lot of homeless people stealing the clothes off our back!

NICK. Are we going on the street...?

DAD. Let's just calm down and let mommy eat her dinner while you describe what happened at school today.

TOM. He hit me ...
NICK. I did not ...
DAD. You didn't hit your brother? You mean the school made mom leave work for no reason at all...?
NICK. It wasn't me.
TOM. It was, too.
DAD. Let him finish. You mean that somebody hit him, but it wasn't you?
NICK. Yes.
TOM. Liar!
DAD. Shhh. Who hit him?
NICK. It was ... Dogbrain ... *(A huge black thing looms up out of Nick's body for a moment. No one sees it. The shadow subsides into Nick again.)*
MOM. All right, that's enough of your stories, Nicholas. No more hitting, scratching, biting or pulling *anyone,* including — *especially* your brother or there will be no TV for a month, no riding your bicycle after school ...
TOM. Bike, bike, can I ride my bike ...
NICK. No you can't ...
TOM. You can't tell me what to do, you're not king of me.
NICK. Shut up, stupid-Tom ... *(The black shadow, Dogbrain, looms up again, grabs Nick's arm and causes it to strike Tom.)*
DAD. Nicholas, I saw that ... you hit him. *(Dogbrain subsides from view.)*
NICK. It was Dogbrain. He *made* me do it.
MOM. All right, Nicholas, time out. Go right to your room for five minutes.
NICK. But, mom, I'm telling you the truth. I can't help it if Dogbrain makes me do stuff ...
MOM. *(At her wit's end.)* What are we going to *do* about your stories, Nicholas? *(Dad waxes sympathetic.)*
DAD. Who is Dogbrain?
TOM. Yeah, who's Dogbrain?
NICK. He's just this sort of dumb old dark thing and he hangs around and hides and then he makes me do these stupid things and I can't help it.
MOM. *(Pointing.)* Room!

NICK. *(Aggrieved.)* Mom!
MOM. To your room, five minutes.
NICK. One more chance, please!
DAD. Take your plate to the sink and go to your room.
NICK. But dad, I haven't finished my dinner, you want me to starve to death?
DAD. One. Two. Three. F —
NICK. OKAY, OKAY, OKAY! *(Nick takes his plate and starts towards the sink. Dogbrain looms up and lumbers along behind [a black spandex sack-type thing, an amorphous creature with white gloved hands, and white lips]. Nick sees everyone watching him.)* I'M GOING TO MY STUPIDEST ROOM IN THE ENTIRE UNIVERSE, OKAY!!!???
MOM. That's it; straight to bed, young man.
NICK. FINE!!! *(Dogbrain makes Nick's arm lift the plate and smash it against the floor. Nick looks at the others, afraid and amazed at himself. Dogbrain silently cracks up while the others ... "freeze." Nick and Tom go and lie down on the floor. Dad sits between them. Mom and Dogbrain exit. We are now in ...)*

Nicholas/Thomas' bedroom.

Dad is just finishing a story. Two helium balloons float from their beds.

DAD. So Commander Nicholas and Teenie Tom hopped on the back of their new friend, Humpback The Whale, and rode the seven seas to become the most swashbuckling adventurer buddies of their time. The end.
NICK. Then what?
TOM. Tell us a venture they had, please, please? *(Mom appears in the door.)*
DAD. "*Ad*-venture." Tomorrow. *(Dad and Mom hug, Dad leaves and Mom kneels, kisses Tom.)*
MOM. 'Night Birthday Boy.
TOM. And Nick can't come to my party, right, 'cause he's too old, right?
MOM. He always invites you to *his* party. He *is* your brother,

after all.

TOM. *(Not happy.)* That doesn't mean he's my friend. *(Mom goes to Nicholas and kisses him goodnight.)*

MOM. And as for *you,* Mister-Imagination Plus with your stories about Doghead ...

NICK. Dog-*brain.* And he's real.

MOM. Sweetie, you're old enough to know the difference between reality and make-believe by now. There is no Dogbrain. 'Night-night. *(She kisses him and leaves.)*

TOM. *(Chants.)*

Nick is a story-teller
Nyah nyah-nyah nyah, nyah!

NICK. I wish you'd never been born butt-face!

TOM. Story teller, story teller
Nyah nyah-nyah nyah, nyah!

NICK. I'll come over there and bonk you on your stupid head if you don't shut up.

TOM. I'll tell mom.

NICK. No you won't. *(Dogbrain leaps into view and bonks Tom on the head.)*

TOM. Owwww!!!

NICK. *(Looking.)* What happened?

TOM. Something owie-ed my head ...

NICK. Well, it couldn't have been me ... I'm way over here, right. *(Tom looks at Nick, confused. He rubs his head.)*

TOM. It felt like you.

NICK. Like how? *(Dogbrain bonks Tom again. Nick is almost afraid to look.)*

TOM. Owww!!!

NICK. Now what?!

TOM. It happened again.

NICK. Another owie? Did it hurt? A lot?

TOM. Something's in the room.

NICK. Only you and me. Shut up and go to sleep. *(Tom lies down. Nick looks across the room at Dogbrain standing over Tom. Dogbrain looks back at him.)*

DOGBRAIN. Should I bonk him again? One more time, just for good luck? *(Nicholas looks away, then looks back at Dogbrain through spread fingers.)*

TOM. What are you doing, Nick?

DOGBRAIN. *(Teasing, sing-song.)* Nicholas, oh Nicholas! You *know* I'm here. Woof-woof. Your brother can't see or hear me.... Only *you* can.

NICK. What do you want?

TOM. Who are you *talking* to?

DOGBRAIN. *(To Nick.)* What do *you* want?

NICK. Dogbrain!?

DOGBRAIN. At your service; woof!

TOM. Not Dogbrain again!!!???

NICK. But I made you up!

DOGBRAIN. And you can make me go away. Which will it be?

NICK. But you're supposed to be inside me.

DOGBRAIN. That's no fun. Inside I can only make *you* do bad stuff, then *you* get in trouble. But if you let me stay out here, I can do all the cool stuff you *feel* like doing, but you'll be like across the room, or at school, or on Mars or something, so no one can say it was *you* who did it and you won't get in trouble.

NICK. You mean like if my brother is driving me crazy because he's being stupid ...

TOM. I am *not* stupid! *(Dogbrain bonks Tom on the head.)* OWWW!!! *(Tom sits bolt upright in bed.)* It happened again. Someone *is* in the room and you're talking to him even though he's ivisible.

NICK. It's *invisible,* stupid. And there's no one else in the room.

DOGBRAIN. See? You can't get in trouble. Because you didn't do anything. *(Dad comes in to check on the noise. While he talks, Dogbrain dances in his face to prove he's invisible.)*

DAD. Hey, what's all the noise in here?!

TOM. I got owied ...

DAD. Have you two been fighting?

NICK. Thomas fell out of bed and bonked his head ... right Tom? Or was it the famous invisible man who did it?

TOM. I fell.

DAD. No more commotion in here, guys. Sleep! *(Dad leaves.*

Nick and Tom are quiet. Dogbrain dances slowly round Nick's bed, chanting:)

DOGBRAIN.

WHATEVER YOU THINK
WHATEVER YOU SAY
WHATEVER YOU WANT ME TO DO
I'LL OBEY
SAY THE MAGIC WORDS SO I CAN STAY ...

Then you'll be king of me, and I'll be your best friend and protector. I'll do the bad stuff, so you never get in trouble!!!.

NICK. You don't do *really* bad stuff, right?

DOGBRAIN. I can only do what you want me to. So, what'll it be; yes, no, stay, go?

TOM. Nick, who are you talkin' to? *(Dogbrain moves to bonk Tom.)*

NICK. Don't! He's scared. Leave him alone.

DOGBRAIN. *(Retreating.)* Your wish is my command; woof!!!

TOM. I know someone's here because you're talking to 'em. Tell me who ... please?

DOGBRAIN. Say the magic words!? *(Nick points to his mouth, pleading that he doesn't want to frighten Tom.)* Don't speak with your mouth; just put your hand on your head and I'll hear your thoughts. *(Nick does this.)*

NICK. What are the magic words?

DOGBRAIN. LORTINO.

NICK. LORTINO?

DOGBRAIN. CANIMA.

NICK. CANIMA?

DOGBRAIN. AYEE ...

NICK. *(Hand off his head.)* LORTINO CAMINA AYEE?

DOGBRAIN. *Think* it, don't *say* it; hand on head, hand on head.

TOM. Lortina camina — *(Dogbrain bonks him.)* Owwwieee.... It happened again. There's a ghost in here ... I want to get in your bed. *(Dogbrain bonks Tom.)*

DOGBRAIN. WOOF!

NICK. Forget it.

TOM. I'll be your best friend and you can always be the

king and decide what we play and you can even come to my birthday.

NICK. Who wants to come to your stupid birthday, anyway. *(Dogbrain bonks Tom.)*

DOGBRAIN. WOOF! *(Tom sobs.)*

TOM. I'm really scared for really really real. Please can I get in your bed?!

NICK. *(Magnanimous.)* O-kay. *(Tom rushes over. Nick hugs him.)* Don't worry, we're alone. You're just imagining things.

TOM. Like you and Dogbrain...?

NICK. Exactly like that.

TOM. Will you do something? Will you bonk me on the head so it's a real person who's doing it then I won't be so a-scared.

NICK. *(Playfully.)* Doink! He bonks Tom, who bonks him back.

TOM. Doink!

NICK. Doink-doink!!!

TOM. Doink-doink!!! *(They roll around on the floor tussling and knocking each other on the head. Mom bursts in.)*

MOM. *What* is the *meaning* of this?!!! *(Dogbrain slips round behind her, lifts her dress and makes a loud rude fart sound.)* WHAT??? *(Nick claps hand to head.)*

NICK. *(Speaking his thought.)* COOL!!! *("Freeze." Nick and Tom sit at the table. Mom serves breakfast. We are now in their ...)*

Dining area.

Tom fidgets, moving things around the tabletop, humming distractedly.

MOM. And when I get home from work tonight I expect to see your room spotless, or there will be no play dates and no bicycle rides in the park, is that clear Nicholas?

NICK. No fair!

MOM. "No fair, no fair," what's no fair?

NICK. I didn't mess up the room, Tom did.

MOM. You *both* did, and you'll both clean it up. Thomas,

did you hear me? *(Tom is oblivious, fidgeting with crockery on the table.)* THOMAS!!!

TOM. *(Puzzled, looking up.)* What?

MOM. Both of you are responsible for cleaning your room, do you understand.

TOM. 'Kay. *(He continues to fiddle around.)*

MOM. Please stop fidgeting. Stop *touching* everything on the table. Sit still. Eat your cereal.

NICK. *(Under his breath.)* Ha-ha, stupid-Tom.

MOM. *(Hearing.)* And I'm holding *you* responsible for the room being clean since you're the oldest. *(Mom puts her coffee cup on the table and returns to the stove.)*

TOM. *(Revenge.)* Nah nah-nah, poo-poo.

NICK. You're in big trouble now. *(Dogbrain leaps into view.)*

DOGBRAIN. You called, woof-woof. *(Nick looks around nervously.)* Don't worry; no one can see, no one can hear. Only you.

NICK. *(Hand on head.)* I *hate* my brother.

DOGBRAIN. Of course you do, he's a jerk.

NICK. *(Hand on head.)* I have to clean the room because *he* got mom all crazy, is that fair? I wish he was in really bad trouble.

DOGBRAIN. Good idea! *(Both look around the room. Nick sees Tom fidgeting. He gets excited and forgets his hand on his head.)*

NICK. I GOT IT!!!

MOM. What do you have, Nicholas? *(Mom and Tom look at him.)*

DOGBRAIN. THINK it. Don't SAY it.

NICK. *(Hand on head.)* I have an idea ...

DOGBRAIN. I know what it is, but you have to get away from the table right now, and leave the rest to me.

MOM. What do you have?

NICK. *(To Mom.)* I have the orange juice ... okay? I'll get the orange juice from the fridge.

MOM. That's very sweet of you. *(Noticing Tom.)* Thomas, stop fidgeting and eat your cereal, don't make me say it again!!! *(Nick goes to the fridge for o.j. while Dogbrain slides the coffee cup across the table. Tom watches, points, speechless. Meanwhile, Mom is kissing Nick's head.)* I know you're a good boy, sweetie. I don't mean to snap at you so much, but this move ... *(Kindly.)* and the two of you are quite a handful, you know. And on top of everything else this new job is just ...

NICK. *I'll* get a job, okay? Then you can stay home and relax.

MOM. You sweetie pie!!! *(She kisses him on the head. Tom finds his voice, pointing.)*

TOM. *(Terrified.)* Mom!

MOM. Just a minute, dear. *(To Nick.)* I love you very very much, you know.

TOM. MOM!!!

MOM. I'm talking to Nicholas, please stop interrupting.

TOM. But the cup is moving ... *(And before Mom can turn Dogbrain pushes it onto the floor.)*

MOM. TOM! WHAT HAVE YOU *DONE!?*

TOM. Nuffin'. It fell down. *(Dogbrain and Nick [behind Mom's back] are silently high-fiving.)*

MOM. *(To Tom.)* ALL RIGHT, THAT'S IT, YOU ARE GOING TO CLEAN YOUR ROOM RIGHT NOW; BY YOURSELF, DO YOU UNDERSTAND?! *(Mom gets a cloth and kneels to wipe the spill.)*

TOM. But mom, I didn't move the cup.

MOM. Room! Now! Not another word. *(Dad enters in his bathrobe.)*

DAD. Morning guys, morning honey. What's going on here? *(On her hands and kneels cleaning, Mom explains, Dad pours coffee.)*

MOM. What does it *look* like. I'm cleaning up after Mister Fuss and Fidget because he just spilled my coffee. Which he would not have done if a certain someone could wake up a little earlier and keep and eye on the kids while I make breakfast.

DAD. *(Teasing.)* The last time I tried you said I was in the way. *(While Mom speaks, Nick watches her bottom, which is stuck out high and swaying while she wipes the floor. Dogbrain also sees. Dad wanders to Mom to look over her shoulder.)*

MOM. Everyone just wanders down whenever they feel like it and expects maid service ...

DOGBRAIN. *(Re: Mom's butt.)* Do you know what *I'm* thinking?

NICK. *(Hand on head.)* GO FOR IT!!! *(Dogbrain pats Mom's bottom.)*

MOM. *What* on *earth* are you doing?! *(Dad, clueless, calmly sips his coffee at the table behind her.)*

DAD. *(Innocently.)* I'm having my coffee.

MOM. This is neither the *time* nor the *place.*

DAD. For coffee? *(Mom shakes her head in disgust. Nick's eyes are huge, excited.)*

MOM. *(Muttering.)* So now it's a joke, is it?! Honest to goodness, one of these days I'm going to stay in bed and let everyone start the day without me, then we'll see how funny it is ... *(Dogbrain rubs Mom's fanny.)* STOP THAT!!! *(Standing abruptly.)* I'm living in a madhouse. No one listens to a word I say.

DAD. Where did *that* come from?

MOM. Just for that, you can make your own breakfast. And you two *(Nick and Tom.)*, up to your room, brush your teeth and get ready for school. *(Mom trounces out, leaving Dad bewildered.)*

TOM. Did somefin' happened?

DAD. You heard your mother. Up, brush, school. *(To Nick.)* Move! *(Tom and Nick go, Nick looking back at Dogbrain, who gestures to him that he can leave. Doubtful, Nick lingers a moment, then leaves with a backward glance. Dad puts down his coffee cup and goes to the "toaster." As he puts two slices in and depresses the lever, Dogbrain carries Dad's coffee cup to the counter and sets it on the opposite end. Nick sticks his head round the corner and watches Dad. Dad returns to the table and sorts through his newspaper, reaching blindly out for the cup. His hand touches nothing, pats the air, gropes blindly, while continuing to peruse his paper. Where's the cup? He looks. On the counter?! How did it get there?! Meanwhile, Dogbrain flips Dad's bread slices from the toaster and leans them together like a tent on the counter. Dad retrieves his coffee cup, then notices his slices for toast out of the toaster, and propped up against each other in a tent?! He did <u>that</u>? He shakes his head, bewildered, and puts the bread back in the toaster. As Dogbrain lifts the newspaper, Nick* *gestures "no, no, no" but Dogbrain puts it* <u>*under*</u> *the table. Dad takes his cup back to the table. Where is his newspaper? He looks around, spots it. To himself.)* Under the table? I put my newspaper *under the table!? (Nick starts to call out "no.")*

DOGBRAIN. Shhh! Not a word! *(Dad, shaking his head, lifts the paper back onto the table, then looks at the toaster, wondering if he'll discover another trick. Meanwhile, Dogbrain puts Dad's coffee cup under the table, chanting to Nick:)*

DOGBRAIN.

> You've *al*ways wanted to *do* this,
> Haven't you,
> Haven't you!?

NICK. *(Doubtful.)* Only sort of ... *(Dad looks at the table. Where is his coffee cup?! This is definitely weird. He is looking around as Mom walks in.)*

MOM. What are you doing?!

DAD. I seem to be forgetting where I put things.

MOM. You're always forgetting where you put things.

DAD. Yes, I'm sure its nothing serious.

MOM. *(Mildly curious.)* Serious? What's serious?

DAD. Nothing. I just ... for some reason I just put my newspaper under the table.

MOM. Under the table?

DAD. When I went to look for it, there it was. Strange.

MOM. It must have dropped on the floor.

DAD. — Then there was my coffee cup. *(Mom sees where it is.)*

MOM. You put your coffee cup under the table?

DAD. Whenever I try to find something, it's not where I thought I left it.

MOM. Darling, you're getting me worried.

DAD. Then I made a tent with my toast, and I don't remember doing it ...

MOM. You're getting me *very* worried. That's exactly how it started with Uncle Terrence.

DAD. Uncle Terrence? The one who went bananas, what's that got to do with me?

MOM. At first he forgot little things, like the days of the

week, then he forgot words for parts of his body and called his fingers tadpoles and his feet cigars and then ...

DAD. Darling, you don't really think that —

MOM. We're not taking any chances. The doctor said they might have saved Uncle Terrence if they caught it sooner.

DAD. But he was your uncle ... why should I be developing an illness that runs in *your* family?

MOM. That's not the point. I want you to have some tests today. This morning. Now. I'll arrange for you to check into the hospital right away ...

NICK. *(Almost leaping into view.)* NO...!

DOGBRAIN. *(Stopping Nick.)* Shhhh!

MOM. *(Thinking Dad spoke.)* Why not?

DAD. Oh, good, *you* heard it, too. I was wondering if I'd started hearing voices in my head on top of everything else.

NICK. *(To Dogbrain, hand on head.)* But he's not sick.

DOGBRAIN. Awww, let him worry. He's always taking mom's side.

MOM. *(To Dad, with concern.)* Come to the phone. We're going to call the doctor *right now. (She leads him off like an invalid. Nick emerges.)*

NICK. *(To Dogbrain.)* I don't *want* them to worry ... not *that* much.

DOGBRAIN. "Clean your room, brush your teeth, stop making up stories, stop hitting your stupid brother." Aren't you sick and tired of them breathing down your neck night and day?

NICK. Sure, but —

DOGBRAIN. Come on ... it's not like they can blame you for anything, can they?

NICK. No.

DOGBRAIN. So lets make *them* sweat for a change!

NICK. You think so?

DOGBRAIN. Don't you?

NICK. *(Finally, with enthusiasm.)* Okay!

DOGBRAIN. Now let's go to school and have some fun.

NICK. *(Finally enthusiastic.)* Cool!!! *("Freeze." Tom runs onstage*

and tags Nick. Playground noises.)
TOM. You're it!!!

Playground at school.

Tom runs off [or around stage] as Nick chases him. Taunting.

TOM. You'll never catch me,
You're too-oo slo-ow!
(Dogbrain lies in Tom's path and trips him. Nick tags Tom.)
NICK. You're it! *(Nick runs around stage taunting Tom.)*
You can't catch me,
Nyah, nyah-nyah poo-poo.
TOM. You can't tag me if I trip, that's a rule.
NICK. It is not a rule, pinhead.
TOM. Ye-es! If you trip someone you can't tag them, that's a famous rule that everyone knows about. *(Dogbrain punctures Tom's balloon. To Nick.)* No fair! You broke my birthday bloot.
NICK. It's not a bloot, it's called a "balloon," and you're not even supposed to bring it to school, stupid-Tom. *(Tom goes up to Nick.)*
TOM. You can't say "stupid." *(He pushes Nick in the chest.)*
NICK. Don't push me, I'm warning you.
TOM. You can't push me back 'cause I'm younger than you and you're spose to teckt me. *(Tom pushes him again.)* Better not touch me or I'll tell everyone how you broke my bloot. *(Tom pushes Nick some more. Finally, Dogbrain pulls Tom's hat down over his eyes.)* HEY!!! *(Tom turns his head this way and that way.)* I can't see nuffin'!
NICK. Hah! *(Tom finally realizes his hat is over his eyes and pulls it up.)*
TOM. That's not funny, stupid-Nick.
NICK. I didn't do anything.
TOM. Yes you did and I'm gonna get you. *(Tom starts towards Nick but Dogbrain pulls down his cap again.)* HEY!!! *(Tom pulls it up, now suspicious. What's going on here?)*
NICK. I'm way over here!
TOM. Then who did it?

DOGBRAIN. Go on! Tell him!

NICK. It's Dogbrain. He'll do whatever I want.

TOM. There *is* no such thing...! He's just 'tend. *(Dogbrain pulls Tom's hat down — hard!)* Why you ... *(Tom tries to pull it up, dancing around the stage until finally — pop, up it comes!)*

NICK. *(Taunting.)* There's no Dogbrain, eh...?!

TOM. Now I'm really going to get you.

NICK. "Now I'm really going to get you!" *(He laughs and steps backwards.)*

TOM. I'm going to tell on you.

NICK. Tell what, stupid-Tom, I didn't do anything.

TOM. I'll tell anyway. I'll say it was you and they'll believe me because everyone knows you're a story-teller.

NICK. You're the story-teller, not me. *(Miss Harmony enters wearing a Walkman, tuning out the world.)*

TOM. Guess who they'll believe...!! Miss Harmony, Nick is being a bully. He tripped me then he pulled my hat down and then he called me a liar ... *(Miss Harmony doesn't hear. She begins to boogaloo a little, then a little more.... Then she's full out dancing.)*

NICK. *(Chanting.)*

She can't hear you,
Nah nah-nah poo poo!!!

TOM. *(Louder.)* Miss Harmony!!! *(Miss Harmony "hears something" and removes her headphones to look. Tom starts to call again, but Dogbrain, standing behind him, claps his hand over Tom's mouth. Tom's eyes register terror as he struggles to speak. Miss Harmony watches Tom, then Nick, then Tom:)*

MISS HARMONY. What are *you* two up to?

NICK. My brother always clowns around. *(Miss Harmony decides it's a case of boys-will-be-boys, and replaces her headphones. She resumes dancing. Dogbrain unclaps Tom's mouth.)*

TOM. What was *that!?*

NICK. I'm king of *MAGIC!* I'm king of the *WORLD.* I'm king of *YOU!!! (With each strong word, Nick makes an aggressive feint towards Tom while Dogbrain actually shoves him backwards, making him more and more fearful until he screams:)*

TOM. MISS HARMONY!!!! *(She hears! She whips off her head-*

phones and spins around.)

MISS HARMONY. What!? *(Just as she turns, Dogbrain pulls down Tom's pants. Miss Harmony sees Tom with his pants down.)* THOMAS! YOU COME TO MY OFFICE RIGHT THIS MINUTE!!! *(Nick claps hand to head.)*

NICK. COOL!!!! *("Freeze." Miss Harmony goes. Tom and Nick sit at the table, eating. We are back in their ...)*

Dining room.

Mom enters, pacing as she reads a note from school.

MOM. According to this note from Miss Harmony, Tommy was terrified by something you did to him, but he wouldn't tell her what it was. Why?

NICK. *(Mr. Innocence.)* I don't know.

MOM. Thomas? *(Dogbrain grabs his earlobe and starts to twist. Tom winces.)*

TOM. Nuffin'.

MOM. Then why did you pull down your pants in front of Miss Harmony?

TOM. I don't know.

MOM. What is going on with you two?

NICK. Nothing.

TOM. Nuffin'.

NICK. You should have never been born is what's happening with you! *(Mom's voice wavers.)*

MOM. I really could use a little co-operation from you two. I can't run this house all on my own ...

TOM. Where's daddy?

MOM. He ... he has to be somewhere for a few days.

TOM. Where? *(Mom decides to make a formal announcement.)*

MOM. All right; Nicholas. Thomas. Daddy is spending the night at a special hospital where they can do some tests on him.

TOM. What *kind* of tests?

MOM. It's just a very simple examination to find out why he's doing certain things.

TOM. What things?

MOM. Oh ... like putting his newspaper under the table. And forgetting where he left his coffee cup. And playing games with his toast.

NICK. *(Blurting.)* That wasn't him, mom ...

MOM. What wasn't...?

DOGBRAIN. You gonna tell her "Dogbrain did it?"

NICK. Nothing, mom.

TOM. Is dad gonna be dead...? *(Mom barely keeps from bursting into tears.)*

MOM. Oh, I hope not, honey. *(Mom hugs Tom.)* Would you two please clear your dishes and take your bath? I'll come in later and read a story. *(She goes. Dogbrain follows her out.)*

TOM. Daddy has to do the story. Not mom.

NICK. He will. As soon as he gets home again.

TOM. But if he gets dead he'll never come home and we'll never have a story again.

NICK. Nothing's wrong with daddy, I promise.

TOM. Cross your heart and hope to die?

NICK. Yes. Now run your bath ... *(Tom leaves. Dogbrain bounds in.)*

DOGBRAIN. Boy is he stupid. I'll pull down his pants again!

NICK. No.

DOGBRAIN. I'll put peanut butter in his shoes!

NICK. No.

DOGBRAIN. How 'bout a turtle in his bed, or thumb tacks in his socks, or chicken soup down his pants so mom thinks he had an accident.... Cool!!!

NICK. Don't do anything. Just ... sit there and be quiet. *(Dogbrain sits. He fidgets.)*

DOGBRAIN. Is that dirt on the floor? Yummie! *(Dogbrain eats some dirt.)* I loooove dirt!!!!

NICK. You're gross.

DOGBRAIN. Hey! I'm your friend. Chill.

NICK. I want to be alone.

DOGBRAIN. Let's set fire to mom's briefcase!

NICK. Why?

DOGBRAIN. To upset her.

NICK. She's already upset.
DOGBRAIN. Let's upset her *more!!!*
NICK. I said no.
DOGBRAIN. But you *thought* "yes."
NICK. You mean you know what I'm *thinking?*
DOGBRAIN. Of course I do.
NICK. Everything?
DOGBRAIN. Sure. Like when you wonder things, like why mom and dad ever wanted another kid, especially one like stupid-Tommy when they already had the greatest kid in the world ... I can hear that. *(Tom peeks in and watches Nick.)*
NICK. And they never believe what I say but they always believe him even when he's lying, and I don't have any friends —
DOGBRAIN. — Except *me.*
NICK. *(Stops.)* I thought I had to do this *(Hand on head.)* so you could hear me think.
DOGBRAIN. Only at first. Not any more.
NICK. I don't like this.
DOGBRAIN. *(Offended.)* Oh boy. Some thanks! You go become someone's best friend, *such* a good friend he doesn't even have to tell you what he's thinking because you already know, and what do you get? "I don't like this ..."
NICK. I want my thoughts to stay inside.
DOGBRAIN. Then why did you let me out?
NICK. I didn't.
DOGBRAIN. Then who *did* it; Dogbrain?
NICK. Wait a minute; now you're getting me all confused.
DOGBRAIN.

WHATEVER YOU THINK
WHATEVER YOU SAY
WHATEVER YOU WANT ME TO DO
I'LL OBEY ...

That was the deal, and you said the magic words, LORTINA CAMINA AYEE, so now I'm out here forever, and nothing can make me go away.... *(Nick covers his ears.)* Let's put Cheerios in the turtle tank. Let's throw Tommy's toys out the window. Let's dump some Mister Clean in the bathwater, a whole *bottle* of Mister Clean — oh, wait, I already did that.

NICK. You did *what? (A scream. Mom comes dashing in.)*
MOM. There's bubbles up to the ceiling! What did you put in the bathtub, Nicholas???!!!
NICK. It wasn't me!!! *(Mom starts out, sobbing. Nick follows after her, upset that she is upset.)* Mom ... *(Not convinced.)* I can explain ...
DOGBRAIN. COOL!!!! *("Freeze." We are now in ...)*

The bedroom.

Tom comes in and lies down. Nick lies down, too. Mom, depressed, kisses them goodnight then looks at them both.

MOM. Please, you two, don't come in my room tonight. I'll see you in the morning. Sleep tight. *(Nick gets out of bed and starts shoving things in a backpack; clothes, a stuffed doggie. Tom watches him. Dogbrain stalks something along the floor.)*
TOM. What are you doing?
NICK. Go to sleep. *(Dogbrain pounces, grabs a spider and gulps it down.)*
DOGBRAIN. Spider, yummy!!
TOM. Are you gonna run away?
NICK. None of your business.
DOGBRAIN. *(Perks up.)* Hey, cool! Running away'll *really* upset everyone. Bug! *(He leaps, gobbles the bug.)* Double yummie — cockroach.
TOM. Are you leaving 'cause of Dogbrain?
NICK. There is no Dogbrain, stupid.
TOM. Yes there is. I heard you talking to him downstairs.
DOGBRAIN. What a jerk. Ants!!! *(Dogbrain licks them off the floor.)*
NICK. You believe me about Dogbrain...?
TOM. Yes. *(Nick draws close to Tom.)*
NICK. *(In a whisper.)* I have to get away so he follows me away from here and stops doing bad stuff to you and mom and dad. He knows what I'm thinking even.
DOGBRAIN. *(Licking.)* This floor is so *filthy* it's deee-licious!
TOM. Where you gonna go?

NICK. Somewhere far away, so Dogbrain can't hurt you guys. *(Dogbrain sees something wonderful on the floor.)*

DOGBRAIN. A dead rat! How did *that* get here? Shares-ies? *(He wrenches it in half and offers it to Nick, who ignores him.)*

TOM. What if you get kidney-lamped by a horrbul baggage person.

DOGBRAIN. It's "kidnapped" stupid, not kidney-lamped.

TOM. Or a big German leopard 'tacks you. *(Nick isn't sure. He looks worried until:)*

DOGBRAIN. I'll just bop 'em in the face ...

NICK. *(Oh, okay.)* I'll just bop them in the face!!!

TOM. You're not afraid?

DOGBRAIN. I'm not afraid of anything.

NICK. I'm not afraid of anything. *(Dogbrain claps him on the back.)*

TOM. Can I come?

DOGBRAIN. Him?! That pinhead, come with US?!!

NICK. You belong here at home. I'm just in the way.

TOM. If you're running away for really real you need money to buy candy and toys and stuff and I saved up about a zillion jillion dollars and you can have half if you let me come. *(Tom empties a canister.)*

NICK. Tell mom that nothing's wrong with dad. Me and Dogbrain played a trick on him.

TOM. 'Kay. *(Nick leaves. Dogbrain looks back at Tom.)*

DOGBRAIN. Bye, butt-head! *(Dogbrain leaps offstage. Thomas watches the door for a moment. He looks sad.)*

TOM. NICK!!! *(Nick returns instantly, as if he's been waiting just outside.)*

NICK. *(With pretend impatience.) What!??*

TOM. Can I come, *please.*

NICK. You're only four years old. You have to be six to run away from home.

TOM. No fair.

NICK. That's the rules. Go to sleep. *(Nick goes. Tom watches the door.)*

TOM. NICK!!! *(Nick reappears instantly.)* I miss you.

NICK. No you don't. All I do is push you around and bonk

you on the head and make you play everything I want to play.

TOM. Yeah, I *hate* when you do that. But I miss you. *(Dogbrain comes in.)*

DOGBRAIN. That stupid brother of yours doesn't make any sense at all!!!

NICK. Just go to bed. Here, you can have my balloon. *(Nick leaves. Dogbrain follows, with a parting shot to Tom.)*

DOGBRAIN. You're so dumb you're dumber than toothpaste. Woof! *(Dogbrain goes. Tom watches the door sadly.)*

TOM. NICK!!! *(Nick appears instantly.)*

NICK. If you don't shut up and let me run away I'll tell mom you're still awake.

TOM. If you let me come I'll clean the room — every Lego and every block and every Brio train track ...

NICK. What about marbles and pennies and stuff?

TOM. 'Kay.

NICK. And you'll feed the turtles two times a day without my reminding you?

TOM. I swear for really really real.

NICK. All right, stupid brother Tom ...

TOM. Can I bring my bloot? *(Dogbrain hops in.)*

DOGBRAIN. It's "balloon," stupid!

NICK. Yes. *(Tom leaps out of bed.)*

DOGBRAIN. Oh, man, don't tell me *he's* coming?! *("Freeze." Nick and Tom ride their bicycles, scared. Dogbrain hippity-hops along in front of them, shadow-boxing, singing tunelessly. We are in ...)*

A street at night.

DOGBRAIN.

HOORAY (HOORAY!)
WE'RE RUNNING AWAY

NICK and DOGBRAIN.

WE'RE RUNNING AWAY
TODAY (TODAY!)

TOM. Where are we going?

NICK. Just ... away, okay? Far away.

DOGBRAIN.

I WONDER WHAT
THEY'LL SAY (THEY'LL SAY?!)
MOM AND DAD
TODAY (TODAY!)
WHEN THEY DISCOVER
WE'VE RUN AWAY
I'LL BET THEY CRY ALL NIGHT AND DAY
HOORAY, HOORAY, HOORAY!!!

TOM. What if we get lost and no one can ever find us again?

DOGBRAIN. What a dumb-dumb!

NICK. I'll take care of you, Tommy.

TOM. What if we get 'tacked by mobsters and dragons?

DOGBRAIN. You think I'm afraid of stuff like that?

NICK. No problem, Tommy ... I'll protect you. *(To Dogbrain, hand on head.)* You're sure about that?

DOGBRAIN. I'll bite their heads off ...

NICK. *(To Tom.)* I'll bite their heads off.

DOGBRAIN. I'll kick them in the behind.

NICK. I'll kick them in the behind!

DOGBRAIN. I'll punch them in the privates and trip them and bang them with a hammer until they turn into mush.

NICK. I'm not afraid of anything.

TOM. When I'm six and two halves and a half I'm gonna be brave like you. *(Nick starts to turn a corner. Tom stops.)*

NICK. Come on; this way!

TOM. Isn't this the street where Mister Dimple lives?

NICK. So what?

DOGBRAIN. Let's leave stupid-Tom behind.

TOM. Doesn't he have a great big German leopard?

NICK. A great big what?

TOM. I'm afraid of them.

DOGBRAIN. He's afraid of everything. Let's get going.

NICK. *(Trying to understand.)* What's a German leopard?

TOM. With big teeth and it barks.

DOGBRAIN. *(Suddenly apprehensive.)* What?

NICK. A German shepherd? *(A huge German shepherd leaps out of the darkness ... Nick and Tom scream and leap on their bikes, pedaling furiously while the shepherd lopes in pursuit, growling and barking.)*

TOM. Look out!!!

NICK. Dogbrain, get him, bang his head, twist his tail! *(Dogbrain has disappeared.)*

TOM. Faster, Nick ...

NICK. Go, go ... he's falling behind, we're losing him! *(They finally outrun the shepherd and stop pedaling.)*

TOM. Is he gone? *(They listen. Dogbrain leaps on, boxing the air.)*

DOGBRAIN. I showed that pitiful pooch a thing or two!

NICK. You ran away.

DOGBRAIN. Me? Never! I pinched his nose, I pulled his tail, I stuck him in the ribs; I'm Super Dogbrain!!!

NICK. You're full of hot air is what you are. You're a coward...!!!

DOGBRAIN. I can beat up a grizzly bear if I feel like it. I can pull airplanes out of the sky —

NICK. Useless, dumb old Dogbrain ...

DOGBRAIN. Woof-woof-woof. *(Nick circles the stage looking for the German shepherd.)*

TOM. I'm hungry.

NICK. Here's an apple.

DOGBRAIN. I'm hungry, too. *(Spots.)* Garbage!!! Cat poop, yummie.

NICK. Gross. *(Nick and Tom sit to eat.)*

TOM. Can you really *see* Dogbrain? For really real?

DOGBRAIN. Wet muddy newspaper, super-delectable!

NICK. I wish I couldn't. I wish he'd go away. He's gross and dumb plus he's a coward.

DOGBRAIN. I'm only what *you* are.

NICK. But I'm other things, too. And you're not.

TOM. Will you let me see him one day?

NICK. I can't.

TOM. Why not?

NICK. That's the rules, okay? I just can't.

TOM. Just tell me why, okay?

DOGBRAIN. I WANT THAT STUPID-TOM TO STOP FLAP-

PING HIS GUMS AND LET ME EAT MY GARBAGE IN PEACE!!! *(Dogbrain bangs Tom repeatedly on the head; hard! Tom yells with pain as Nick calls out!!!)*

NICK. Stop it. *(Dogbrain doesn't stop.)* I said "stop it." He's afraid, don't hit him ... *(Tom runs and hides somewhere.)* Why didn't you stop when I said stop?!

DOGBRAIN. You always let me when I was *inside* you!

NICK. I couldn't see what it looked like.

DOGBRAIN. *(Taunting.)* "I couldn't see what it looked like!"

NICK. The rule is supposed to be you have to do what I want you to. If I say stop, you have to stop.

DOGBRAIN. You *said* stop, but you thought "Hit him!" Thought is a "want-to." The rule is I do what you *want to do.*

NICK. I don't like these rules.

DOGBRAIN. Tough bananas. *(Nick looks around. He can't see Tom.)*

NICK. Tom? *(Calls.)* TOM!!!

DOGBRAIN. *(Spots.)* Ooooo, a slimy rat ... yum-yummie-yum!!! *(Dogbrain stalks the rat. Tom peeks out.)*

TOM. Is *he* still here? *(Dogbrain pounces and stuffs the huge rat into his mouth, chomping with exaggeration.)*

NICK. *(Disgusted.)* He's *still* here.

DOGBRAIN. *(Pointing to his mouth.)* I wish he'd stop moving around in my mouth, dumb old rat.

TOM. Take me home.

NICK. Please stay with me.

TOM. I don't like being owied.

NICK. I don't want to be alone. I'm sorry I ever hit you. I'm sorry I ever hit anyone. I'm sorry I ever thought up Dogbrain.

DOGBRAIN. That was the most succulent rodent I ever ate. If I could add some dead goldfish on a piece of moldy rotten bread and put the rat *between* it; Mmm, a dead-rat and stinky-goldfish sandwich!!!

NICK. Please go away Dogbrain.

TOM. Please take me home, Nick.

NICK. In the morning, okay? Just spend one night. We'll put our bikes behind the wall and pull some garbage cans

around us so no one knows we're here and then we'll be safe.
DOGBRAIN. Garbage?! Did someone say "garbage?"
TOM. My bloot's gone. I want to go home ...
DOGBRAIN. "Balloon, stupid-Tom." *(Tom starts to cry.)*
NICK. I'll get you another bloot tomorrow. And I'll tell you a bedtime story, just like dad.
TOM. Okay ... *(They walk their bikes behind the wall.)*
DOGBRAIN. Hey, what's going on?
NICK. Lie down right there.
TOM. What if someone finds us, like a baggage person.
DOGBRAIN. Bag! Bag! It's "bag-person!!!"
NICK. This time *I'll* protect you.
TOM. Promise?
NICK. Yeah. Lie down, okay?
DOGBRAIN. Would somebody mind telling me what this is all about? *(Nick and Tom lie down.)*
NICK. This is a story about when Nick and Tom ran away from home ...
DOGBRAIN. Let's do something bad.
TOM. Where did they go?
NICK. Oh, Dogville, Oyster Bay, Bear Mountain ...
TOM. I'm a-scared of bears.
DOGBRAIN. Let's let the air out of every tire on the street.
NICK. They went to Heaven, too. And guess what they found there?
TOM. I give up.
NICK. Tom's balloon.
TOM. *(Pleased.)* For real?
DOGBRAIN. Excuse me, over here, guys.
NICK. Where do you think balloons go when you let go of them? They float up to Heaven, of course? The sky there is all balloons, every color, and the strings hang down so you can just reach up and grab the one you want.
TOM. Cool!
DOGBRAIN. I'm *talking* to you, Nicholas.
NICK. And I'm *ignoring* you, Dogbrain.
DOGBRAIN. Oh, yeah?! You can't do that.
NICK. Just watch me ...

TOM. I like this story. It's almost as good as daddy tells.

DOGBRAIN. If you try to shut me out I'll do something loud and bang-ie to make you look, something like ... *(Dogbrain bangs the garbage can lid, LOUD! A Bag Person enters, muttering to him/herself, ferocious-looking.)*

BAG PERSON. What was *that? (Nick and Tom look up, frozen.)*

TOM. Did you *hear* somefin'?

BAG PERSON. Is there a little kitty cat on *my* street stealing food from *my* garbage cans?

TOM. Is it a mobster?

DOGBRAIN. Monster-monster-monster, you yoyo!!!

NICK. Shhhh ... *(Dogbrain lifts the garbage can lid.)*

DOGBRAIN. Want me to make another bang so the monster can see where you are?!!

NICK. No!

DOGBRAIN. Are you *ever* going to ignore me again?

NICK. Never!

DOGBRAIN. That's more like it.

BAG PERSON. Maybe it's a cute little puppy dog trying to steal my garbage. Maybe I'll have to pick you up and smash you on the ground until your little spine breaks in two pieces, snap!

TOM. *(To Nick.)* He's coming closer.

NICK. *(Whisper.)* Dogbrain, help us.

BAG PERSON. I'm going to find you *any* minute, I'm getting closer, closer, closer ...

TOM. I have to sneeze.

NICK. Hold it in ... Dogbrain, do something!

DOGBRAIN. *(Cowering.)* I'm formulating a plan ...

NICK. *(Seeing him clearly.)* You're not formulating anything. You're *scared.*

DOGBRAIN. *Excusez-moi?* Dogbrain, *scared?!!*

NICK. Some protector you turned out to be! You're full of baloney is what you are. Plus you're a liar and a bully and a creep.

DOGBRAIN. Oh yeah? Oh yeah?

TOM. I can't stop my ... sneeze, A-CHOO!!!

BAG PERSON. *(Spins around.)* That was not a little-kitty noise. That was not a little-puppy noise. That was a little *person* noise. This is *my* street. Who is stealing from my garbage cans?!
TOM. It's a baggage-person.
NICK. Shhhh!!! *(Dogbrain hides. The Bag Person gets:)*
BAG PERSON. Closer … closer … I'm *very* warm now, aren't I? *These* cans don't look right. *(The Bag Person throws them aside. Dogbrain runs squealing away. Tom screams. Nick gasps. They crouch before the Bag Person and quake with terror.)* Little people on my street. Little people stealing my garbage.
NICK. I wasn't.
BAG PERSON. *(Points to Tom.) He* was.
TOM. No!
BAG PERSON. He has an apple in his hand and it's half-eaten. It's mine …
TOM. Nick gave it to me …
BAG PERSON. You *lie,* little person…. It's *my garbage!* MINE!!! Give it back!!! *(The Bag Person starts after Tom. Nick looks around, frantic.)*
NICK. Dogbrain, we really need help; where are you? *(Tom is cornered.)*
BAG PERSON. Time to snap some spines … *(He/she reaches out for Tom.)*
TOM. No … get away from me!!! Don't. Nick, help!!!
NICK. *(Grabbing the Bag Person.)* Leave him alone. *(The Bag Person turns on Nick.)*
BAG PERSON. *What* did you *say?!*
NICK. He's my brother. If you lay one hand on him …
BAG PERSON. You'll *what?! (Nick thinks frantically.)*
NICK. You're looking for food, right? So you must be hungry and I have a whole apple. If you leave him alone you can have it.
BAG PERSON. You have a whole, entire, uneaten apple?
NICK. And … and chocolate milk, and a sandwich. I packed enough for one whole year when we ran away.
BAG PERSON. Let me see! *(Nick shows him the food.)* A whole year's worth, eh?

TOM. Maybe more if we chew slow.

BAG PERSON. You ran away from home?

NICK. Yes.

BAG PERSON. Why?

NICK. I'm just a lot of trouble at home.

BAG PERSON. You're a kid. You're *supposed* to be trouble.

NICK. Not all the time.

BAG PERSON. Why did *you* run away?

TOM. He's my brother. He's my best friend. I go with him.

BAG PERSON. If you have a brother who's your best friend and a home to go to, go home. You'll stop causing trouble one day. Then you'll grow up and have kids and *they*'ll cause trouble. *(Cackles.)* Now get going or I'll call the police and they'll arrest you and drag you home and then there'll be *real* trouble. Got it?!

NICK. Yes.

TOM. 'Kay ...

BAG PERSON. You don't want to end up on the street like ... some people I could name. *(Nick holds out the paper bag, and Tom holds out his apple.)*

NICK. Take our food.

BAG PERSON. Thank you. Now I can go to sleep with a full belly, just like people with homes, and brothers. *(The Bag Person leaves, checking his/her bag. Dogbrain leaps on stage, calling after him.)*

DOGBRAIN. What a stupid old bum!

NICK. He was not stupid. He was nice. You're the stupid one. You're completely dumb is what you are.

TOM. *(To Dogbrain.)* You're 'dicilous.

NICK. You can *see* him?

TOM. No.

NICK. So who are you talking to?

TOM. *(Thinks.)* I don't know. Same as *you. (Nick laughs.)*

NICK. You're pretty funny, you know that? I guess I'm not *really* sorry you were born ...

DOGBRAIN. Yuck.

NICK. And you really *are* sort of my best friend, I guess.

DOGBRAIN. Double yuck.
TOM. Even though you hate me?
DOGBRAIN. YEAH!
NICK. *(Smiles.)* Yeah. *(Tom leans over.)*
TOM. Is Dogbrain still there? *(Dogbrain whacks him on he head.)* Owww!!!
DOGBRAIN. Three guesses, the first two don't count.
NICK. He's always there ... I can't make him go away.
TOM. Why not?
DOGBRAIN. *(Searching cans.)* Garbage, garbage, I see garbage —
NICK. 'Cause I said magic words to make him stay.
TOM. Say other ones. Go away ones.
NICK. I don't *know* any "go away" ones ...
DOGBRAIN. *(Breezy.)* No such thing, no such thing ...
TOM. Remember in school how they said everything has to have a possipit? Like how hot is the possipit of cold?
NICK. "Opposite?"
TOM. Yeah, possipit! Who told you the magic words to make Dogbrain stay?
NICK. Dogbrain, of course.
TOM. So what's the possipit of Dogbrain?
DOGBRAIN. No such thing, no such thing.
NICK. Puppy-foot?
DOGBRAIN. No such thing ...
TOM. Woof-toes?
DOGBRAIN. No such thing ...
NICK. Maybe Catbrain?
DOGBRAIN. No such thing ...
TOM. Cat-*butt?!*
DOGBRAIN. Yeah, right; that sounds a lot like Goodybags, doesn't it, dumb-face. *(Dogbrain, realizing he's spilled the beans, claps hand over mouth.)*
NICK. Goodybags!?
TOM. Goodybags...!?
DOGBRAIN. Don't say that word.
NICK. What word; you mean Goodybags?

DOGBRAIN. No more, that's enough.

NICK. *(Taunting.)* Goodybags, Goodybags, Goodybags ...

DOGBRAIN. Stop it right this minute ...

TOM. What's happening?

NICK. I don't know, but he hates when I say Goodybags ...

DOGBRAIN. That's seven times, you have to stop ...

NICK. Say Goodybags ...

DOGBRAIN. No, no, that's eight!

TOM. Good-y-bags!

NICK. That's nine ...

DOGBRAIN. No more, please; I'll do whatever you say, I'll do *only* what you say, not what you think, and I'll protect you from everything bad and I'll help clean your room and be nice to your stupid-brother-Tom if you insist!!!

NICK. I think it's the TENTH time he's worried about. *(With a flourish.)* GOODYBAGS!!! *(Goodybags appears from inside Nick. He's shaped like Dogbrain, but instead of black and white, he's yellow, with red lips and gloves.)*

GOODYBAGS. *(Looks around.)* Ahah! Dogbrain! I've been *looking* for you!

DOGBRAIN. Yoiks!!! *(Dogbrain scampers off.)*

NICK. *(To Goodybags.)* Who are you?

TOM. There's *another* one?

GOODYBAGS. That Dogbrain's been quite the trouble-maker lately. Since he got out here there's just no keeping him under control.

NICK. Who are *you?*

TOM. Who is who?

GOODYBAGS. I'll give you a clue. I come from the same place as Dogbrain.

NICK. Inside me?

GOODYBAGS. Right the first time. And I'm here because ...

NICK. Because why?

TOM. 'Cause why ...

GOODYBAGS. Didn't you get sick and tired of Dogbrain and tell him to go back but he wouldn't listen?

NICK. Yes.

GOODYBAGS. And isn't he the one who does all the bad things?

NICK. Yes.

TOM. *(Trying to be part of whatever it is.)* Yes ...

GOODYBAGS. Okay, if you want him to go away, and he's the bad guy, and you call on me to help you; what am I?

TOM. *(Seeing Nick about to speak.)* Yes ...

NICK. The *good* guy. You're the — are you "Goodybags?"

TOM. Nick, what's going on, what's a Goodybags, where's Dogbrain?

NICK. He's a coward. He ran away.

TOM. Then who are you talking to?

GOODYBAGS. Is your brother blind? Can't he see I'm not Dogbrain?

NICK. How could he? Dogbrain's invisible and so are you. *(Beat.)* Aren't you?

GOODYBAGS. That's up to you.

NICK. It is...?

GOODYBAGS. Hmmmm, very interesting. You never let him see the bad guy. I like that. But why wouldn't you want him to see your good guy buddy?

NICK. I didn't know I could.

GOODYBAGS. It's easy as pie. Watch this! *(Goodybags covers Tom's eyes from behind.)*

TOM. Hey, everything's ivisible!

NICK. Don't worry, it's Goodybags, he won't hurt you.

GOODYBAGS. Okay, now say my name ten times ...

NICK. Goodybags, Goodybags, Goodybags, Goodybags, Goodybags, Goodybags, Goodybags, Goodybags, Goodybags, Goodybags ... *(Tom joins in the final few times.... Goodybags takes his hands away from Tom's eyes and presents himself.)*

GOODYBAGS. Taa-daaah!!! *(Tom freaks out, screams and rushes into Nick's arms.)*

NICK. It's okay, he's the good guy. He's going to help us get rid of Dogbrain ...

TOM. Where *is* Dogbrain?

GOODYBAGS. Hiding. He's afraid of me. IN FACT, HE'S

AN ALL ROUND COWARD, AREN'T YOU, DOGBRAIN. He's somewhere nearby, watching us.
NICK. How do we catch him?
GOODYBAGS. We'll set a trap. First we make a pile of everything he likes best ... and when he comes to eat it, we nab him.
NICK. If he's watching, won't he know what we're up to?
GOODYBAGS. The thing about Dogbrain; even when he knows better, he can't control himself.

(AUDIENCE PARTICIPATION VERSION.)

(Goodybags continues.) Okay, let's start our pile; what are some of the things Dogbrain loves ... *(Nick and Tom also elicit the audience, and whatever they suggest [cat poop, cockroaches, etc.] actors suggest.)*
NICK, TOM and GOODYBAGS. How does a cockroach go? How does cat poop go? *(When this is done, Goodybags steps forward.)*
GOODYBAGS. Okay, here comes Dogbrain. Let's hide. *(And all hide, while Dogbrain emerges from concealment and circulates around the audience eating from various segments of the audience.)*

(NON-PARTICIPATION VERSION.)

NICK. I know one thing that Dogbrain loves.
NICK, TOM and GOODYBAGS. MUD!!!
GOODYBAGS. Yes, mud, mud, mud ... *(They make a pile, naming what they find. Dogbrain, nearby, raises his head, watching.)*
DOGBRAIN. Mud ... mmmm!!!
NICK. Filthy mud with bugs in it ...
DOGBRAIN. Bugs, oh bugs...!!!
TOM. Oh, look, mondo-yuck ... a dead squirrel ...
DOGBRAIN. Dead squirrel ... slurp!
GOODYBAGS. Broken glass and wet newspaper ...
NICK. Dog barf ...

TOM. Pigeon doo-doo ...

NICK. Insects!

TOM. Snails and germans ...

NICK. Germs, you dummit. *(This time it's friendly, and both laugh. Dogbrain is swooning with appetite.)*

GOODYBAGS. That's enough, now let's hide!!! *(They hide. Dogbrain peeks round from where he's hiding. He longs to feast.)*

DOGBRAIN. You think you can trap me so easily, Goodybags? With a little mud ... and worms ... and a dead squirrel ... and dog ... barf — *(He swoons with appetite, then controls himself.)* No way. I'm not about to be caught just because I can't resist a few ... insects ... oh baddie; dead worms, dead worms ... *(Dogbrain can't resist. He leaps out and starts to feed noisily.)*

GOODYBAGS. Now!!! *(Nick and Goodybags grab him. Tom tries.)*

NICK. Gotcha, big guy.

TOM. Where *is* he? *(Dogbrain struggles.)*

DOGBRAIN. Let ... me ... go ... you big yellow sack of goody-poody-woody yuckos.

GOODYBAGS. Quick, count to ten backwards, NOW!!!

NICK. Ten-nine-eight-seven-six-five-four-three-two-one. *(Tom joins in the final numbers. Dogbrain "freezes.")*

DOGBRAIN. NO FAIR!!!

GOODYBAGS. He says that all the time. Okay, Dogbrain, you're coming back inside.

DOGBRAIN. You can't make me!

GOODYBAGS. But *he* can.

DOGBRAIN. *(Chant.)* Too late, too late,
He said the magic words!

GOODYBAGS. Well then, he'll just have to unsay them.

DOGBRAIN. *(Chant.)* He'll never remember what they are,
Never, never, never ...

GOODYBAGS. Do you remember the magic words, Nick?

TOM. *What* magic words?

NICK. *(Trying.)* Ummm ...

DOGBRAIN. *(To distract him.)* Bloogah, blaagha, bleegha ... he'll never remember ...

NICK. Be quiet, you ...

(AUDIENCE PARTICIPATION VERSION.)

(Nick asks the audience.) Who remembers the magic words? *(He tries each suggestion, but Dogbrain woofs back, mocking his efforts. Both "participation" and "non-participation" versions resume with:)*

(NON-PARTICIPATION VERSION.)

TOM. Do you mean LORTINO CANIMA AYEEE ... I heard you say that.
DOGBRAIN. Stupid-Tom!!!
NICK. Hey ... thanks, Tom. LORTINO CANIMA AYEEE.... He's still here.
GOODYBAGS. That's not enough. You have to know *how* to say the magic words ...
DOGBRAIN. *(Chants.)* You're not allowed to tell him,
Nyah, nyah-nyah poo-poo ...

(AUDIENCE PARTICIPATION VERSION.)

NICK. Who knows how to say the magic words? Can anyone help me? Please? *(Nick tries any suggestions offered — "upside down?" He stands on his head. "Very fast." He speaks fast. "Very slow." He speaks slow — and so on. If the audience suggests "backwards," go straight to Dogbrain's asterisk-ed line further down.)*

(NON-PARTICIPATION VERSION.)

GOODYBAGS. I'm allowed to give one clue, though; Dogbrain always does the opposite of what he should, right?
NICK. Right ...
GOODYBAGS. So you have to say the words — *(What?)*
NICK. Opposite?

TOM. Upside down?
*NICK. Backwards? *(Realizing.)* BACKWARDS!!!
DOGBRAIN. Noooo!!!! *(Distracting.)* Blaagha-bloogah-bleegah ...
NICK. *(Concentrating fiercely.)* AYE ... YI? I? *(That's it!)* I. CANIMA ... AMIMAC...? AMINA ... AM IN? I AM IN. LORTINO ... ONITROL? ONTROL? Oh, the "KH" from CANIMA. CONTROL!!! I AM IN CONTROL!!!
GOODYBAGS. Yes!!!
DOGBRAIN. Well, woof-woof to all of you.
NICK. That was it!
GOODYBAGS. Come along, you pitiful pooch. We're taking a trip back inside Mister Nicholas.
DOGBRAIN. Stupid humans. Stupid kids ...
GOODYBAGS. And from now on, you're King of Him and King of Me; which makes you King of your Whole Self. Whenever he starts to act up, just say my name ten times ... and I'll take care of him.
NICK. I am in control.... Cool!!! *(Goodybags drags Dogbrain back inside Nick. Tom watches with an open mouth.)*
DOGBRAIN. I really hate when this happens ...
TOM. Is Dogbrain gone, for really real? *(Nick and Tom are alone.)*
NICK. Yeah. It's just you and me now. For really really real. Let's go home ...
TOM. 'Kay. *("Freeze." Nick and Tom suddenly begin to hurry out of their clothes. And we are back in ...)*

The bedroom.

Nick and Tom race to hide beneath their covers.

Hurry up, I hear mom coming ...
NICK. *(Listens.)* That's not mom, that's ... *(A knock on the door.)*
NICK and TOM. Dad!!! *(They snuggle under their blankets, dressed.)*

NICK. Come in!!! *(Dad enters.)*

DAD. Come on, lazy bones, time for breakfast!

TOM. I thought you were in the hospital.

DAD. Just some tests. My head's fine. Clean as a whistle. *(Mom peers in, woozy.)*

MOM. Hey, what am I missing? I thought everyone wanted some waffles with strawberries and whip cream for the special birthday breakfast ... *(Nick and Tom leap out of bed.)*

NICK and TOM. Yea!!! Waffles!!!

DAD. Hey, they have their clothes on already. They got up and dressed all by themselves.

MOM. And put on the same thing they wore yesterday, dirt and all. Honestly!

TOM. No, we ran away and then we came home. *(Nick glowers.)*

NICK. No. It's just a story I told him. *(Mom and Dad exchange a look.)*

MOM. Well, I hope so. If either of you ever ran away it would break our heart.

NICK. Even if it was me?

MOM. Sweetie pie, we love you more than anything in the world.

NICK. More than Tom?

MOM. No. But Tommy's out of this world. You both are! *(Mom snuggles them both.)*

DAD. Why do you think we had another child? If you hadn't been so wonderful we'd have never taken the chance. We got lucky twice.

MOM. Now come on, guys, waffles ... *(To Tom.)* Happy birthday, sweetie.

NICK. *(The good sport.)* Happy birthday. *(Mom and Dad leave. Nick turns to Tom.)* Why did you have to tell them about running away, you dumb-head?!

TOM. I'm not a dumb-head, *you*'re a dumb-head. *(Dogbrain appears, grabs Nick's arm and is about to make him hit Tom.)*

NICK. Goodybags, Goodybags, Goodybags, Goodybags, Goodybags, Goodybags, Goodybags, Goodybags, Goodybags, Goodybags! *(Goodybags looms up and grabs Dogbrain back inside Nick.)*

TOM. You didn't hit me!

NICK. *(Amazed.)* It worked!

TOM. Hey ... you want to come to my birthday party?

NICK. I said his name ten times and ... it worked.

TOM. Please come?

NICK. *(Mock-outraged.)* Me? Come to *your* birthday party? Of course I'll come, not-stupid-Tom-most-of-the- time!

TOM. COOL!!!

MOM. *(Off.)* WAFFLES!!!

NICK and TOM. WE'RE COMING!!! *(They giggle. Nick puts his arm around Tom's shoulder and they exit.)*

THE END

PROPERTY LIST

Dinner plates with food (MOM, NICK)
2 helium balloons (NICK, TOM)
Dining table items (TOM)
Coffee cups (MOM, DAD, DOGBRAIN)
Cloth (MOM)
Coffee pot (DAD)
2 slices of bread (DAD)
Toaster (DAD)
Newspaper (DAD, DOGBRAIN)
Hat (TOM, DOGBRAIN)
Walkman with earphones (MISS HARMONY)
Note from school (MOM)
Bugs: spider, ant, bug (DOGBRAIN)
Dead rat (DOGBRAIN)
Canister with money (TOM)
Bicycles (NICK, TOM)
Rat (DOGBRAIN)
Paper bag with food (NICK)
Apple (TOM)
Mud (NICK, TOM, GOODYBAGS)

SOUND EFFECTS

Playground noises

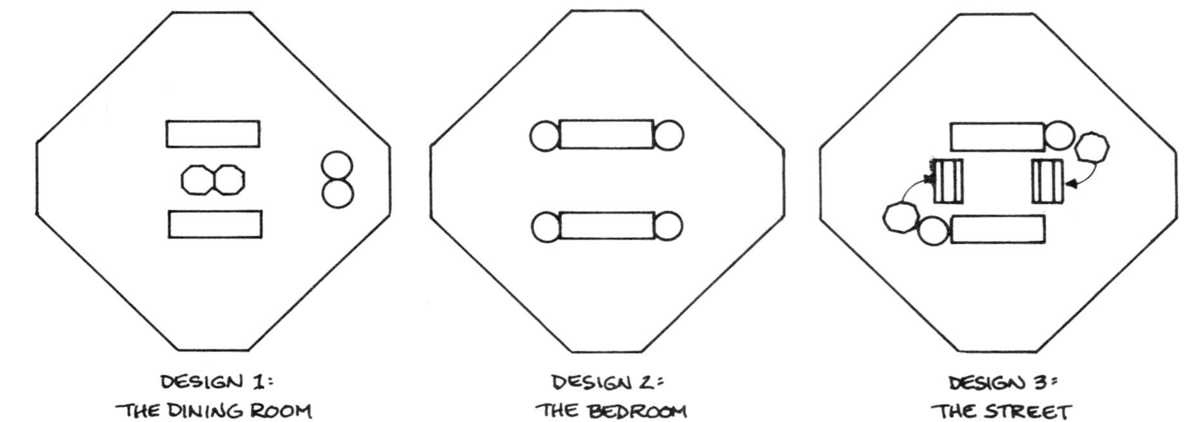

SCENE DESIGN

"DOGBRAIN"

(DESIGNED BY DANIEL S. MANGAN FOR STAGE ONE
AT ACTORS THEATRE OF LOUISVILLE)